# Emotional Correlates of Non-suicidal Self-Injury

Li Miu Ting

# Emotional Correlates of Non-suicidal Self-Injury

## Among Chinese Adolescents in Hong Kong

**LAP LAMBERT Academic Publishing**

**Impressum/Imprint (nur für Deutschland/only for Germany)**
Bibliografische Information der Deutschen Nationalbibliothek: Die Deutsche Nationalbibliothek verzeichnet diese Publikation in der Deutschen Nationalbibliografie; detaillierte bibliografische Daten sind im Internet über http://dnb.d-nb.de abrufbar.
Alle in diesem Buch genannten Marken und Produktnamen unterliegen warenzeichen-, marken- oder patentrechtlichem Schutz bzw. sind Warenzeichen oder eingetragene Warenzeichen der jeweiligen Inhaber. Die Wiedergabe von Marken, Produktnamen, Gebrauchsnamen, Handelsnamen, Warenbezeichnungen u.s.w. in diesem Werk berechtigt auch ohne besondere Kennzeichnung nicht zu der Annahme, dass solche Namen im Sinne der Warenzeichen- und Markenschutzgesetzgebung als frei zu betrachten wären und daher von jedermann benutzt werden dürften.

Coverbild: www.ingimage.com

Verlag: LAP LAMBERT Academic Publishing GmbH & Co. KG
Dudweiler Landstr. 99, 66123 Saarbrücken, Deutschland
Telefon +49 681 3720-310, Telefax +49 681 3720-3109
Email: info@lap-publishing.com

Herstellung in Deutschland:
Schaltungsdienst Lange o.H.G., Berlin
Books on Demand GmbH, Norderstedt
Reha GmbH, Saarbrücken
Amazon Distribution GmbH, Leipzig
ISBN: 978-3-8454-7731-2

**Imprint (only for USA, GB)**
Bibliographic information published by the Deutsche Nationalbibliothek: The Deutsche Nationalbibliothek lists this publication in the Deutsche Nationalbibliografie; detailed bibliographic data are available in the Internet at http://dnb.d-nb.de.
Any brand names and product names mentioned in this book are subject to trademark, brand or patent protection and are trademarks or registered trademarks of their respective holders. The use of brand names, product names, common names, trade names, product descriptions etc. even without a particular marking in this works is in no way to be construed to mean that such names may be regarded as unrestricted in respect of trademark and brand protection legislation and could thus be used by anyone.

Cover image: www.ingimage.com

Publisher: LAP LAMBERT Academic Publishing GmbH & Co. KG
Dudweiler Landstr. 99, 66123 Saarbrücken, Germany
Phone +49 681 3720-310, Fax +49 681 3720-3109
Email: info@lap-publishing.com

Printed in the U.S.A.
Printed in the U.K. by (see last page)
ISBN: 978-3-8454-7731-2

Abstract

**Objective:** The present study examines the emotional correlates of non-suicidal self-injury behavior among Chinese adolescents in Hong Kong. **Method:** A total of 5423 high school students (52.8% females and 47.2% males, aged between 12 and 20 years) completed a self-reported questionnaire assessing negative emotions, emotional reactivity, distress tolerance, impulsivity, and NSSI in class. **Results:** Findings revealed that 31.1% of participants had engaged in NSSI in the past year. Gender differences on emotional correlates, NSSI frequency, methods of NSSI, suicidal ideation/attempt were found. Unique predictive ability of anger and dysphoric mood on NSSI frequency, suicidal ideation and attempt were small. NSSI frequency was the most important predictor for suicidal ideation and attempt. Gender differences on predictive power of emotional variables were also observed. **Discussion:** Findings of the present study contributed to the understandings of predictive ability of emotional correlates, and the associated gender differences on NSSI behaviors.

## Acknowledgements

I am heartily thankful to my supervisor, Prof. Freedom Leung, for his patient guidance, support, and invaluable advice from the initial to the final level in the preparation of my thesis. It has been a great honor and privilege for me to study under his guidance and encouragement. Without his invaluable suggestions and modifications, this thesis would not have been possible.

I am indebeted to Ms. YOU, Jianing, for all the comments, advice and unconditioned assistance through the beginning to the end. I would also like to thank Ms. LI, Tianyuan and Mr. JIA, Shuwei, for their precious suggestions on data analysis and patient tutorship on statistics.

Lastly, I offer my heartfelt regards and blessings to all of those who supported and guided me during the preparation of thesis.

## Table of Contents

List of Tables

Chapter 1

INTRODUCTION

Non-suicidal self-injury (NSSI) was identified as becoming a significant public health

problem among 14% to 15% of adolescents (Ross & Heath, 2002). Given that NSSI served

multiple reasons and the principle of equifinality, it was not surprising that diverse groups of

injurers were present in NSSI.

*Definitions of Non-Suicidal Self-Injury (NSSI)*

Non-suicidal self-injury (NSSI) refers to "a purposeful intention of hurting oneself

without intentionally trying to kill oneself" (Jacobson & Gould, 2007), and was a "direct,

deliberate, self-inflicted destruction of body tissues" (Favazza, 1998; Nock, 2010). Herpetz

(1995) also referred NSSI as "voluntary physical self-injury" which provided a "relatively

immediate non-fatal consequence". NSSI behaviors should be "outside the context of socially

or medically sanctioned procedures" (Briere & Gil, 1998). The deliberate and voluntary

nature in NSSI suggested a conscious intention to directly injure oneself, whereas the

"intention" was not to kill oneself. Though without lethal intention, NSSI could still result in

severe harm or fatality.

NSSI was investigated with diverse wordings in literatures. Common wordings were

self-mutilation (Andover, Pepper, Ryavchenko, Orrico, & Gibb, 2005), self-harm (Milnes,

Owens, & Blenkiron, 2002), self-injurious behavior (Sakelliadis, Papadodima, Sergentanis,

Giotakos, & Spiliopoulou, 2009). Use of diverse wordings give rise to discords in inclusion

criteria and operational definition of NSSI, which perhaps swayed the findings on prevalence

of NSSI across various research.

*Types of NSSI Behaviors*

Diverse types of NSSI behaviors were investigated in previous research. Some examined

a range of NSSI behaviors, though the term for particular type of NSSI might differ (Brown,

Williams, & Collins, 2007; Schroeder, Mulick, & Rojahn, 1980). Range of NSSI behaviors

mainly included cutting, carving, skin picking, punching, scraping skin, bitting, inserting

objects under skin, burning, pulling hair, erasing skin, scratching, head banging. Some

investigated specific type of NSSI, including cutting (Suyemoto & Macdonald, 1995; Yip,

2005; Swenson, Spirito, Dyl, Kittler, & Hunt, 2008; Matsumoto, Yamaguchi, Chiba, Asami,

Iseki, & Hirayasu, 2004; Kumar, Pepe, & Steer, 2004); self-poisoning (Hawton & Fagg,

1992; Greg Carter, Reith, & Whyte, 2005); burning (Thombs, Bresnick, & Magyar-Ruseell,

2007); and skin picking (Calikusu, Yucel, Polat, & Baykal, 2002; Lochner, Simeon, Niehaus,

& Stein, 2002; Wilhelm et al, 1999; Neziroglu & Mancebo, 2001; Keuthen et al, 2000).

Milnes et al (2002) suggested self-poisoning as the most highly endorsed method (89%),

whereas Sakelliadis et al (2009) suggested head banging, writ cutting and skin piercing were

the most common methods. Nock and Prinstein (2004) reported that cutting or carving,

wound picking, punching, scraping skin and biting were the most common methods. Brown et al (2007) found that sticking, scratching, cutting, head banging, and carving were the most

common methods. Though prevalence of NSSI methods and ranking varied across studies,

cutting, burning, biting, punching, and banging were among the five most common types of

NSSI among adolescents.

*Functions of NSSI*

NSSI serves multiple functions. Previous research suggested several models in

explaining NSSI. Suyemoto (1998) suggested six perspectives of NSSI, with affect-regulation

as a function related to anger and dysphoric mood. Klonsky (2007) suggested seven functions

of NSSI, with affect regulation and self-punishment as functions to cope with distress and

expression of anger or derogation to self respectively. The eight functional models of

Suyemoto and Macdonald (1995) identified expression and control as two functions to

express externalized anger and to control mood or anger respectively. Hostility reduction

model of Ross and Heath (2003) alluded releasing anger and redirecting social aggression as

two of the functions in NSSI. Automatic functions, emotional regulation, and social

functions, interpersonal functions were identified as reasons for NSSI as well. In the

assessment of NSSI in Nock and Prinstein (2004), automatic-negative reinforcement (eg., to

get rid of bad feelings/thoughts), automatic-positive reinforcement (eg., to achieve desirable

feelings), social-negative reinforcement (eg., to avoid undesirable social demands), and

social-positive reinforcement (eg., to achieve attention/help from others) were the four major functions of NSSI.

*Possible Subtypes of NSSI*

Previous research mostly studied NSSI without identifying subtypes in NSSI, while some suggested subgroups classified by psychological correlates, materials, locations, frequency, severity, intent to hide, feelings and functions (Kumar et al, 2004). For example, one might pick the skin on areas like face, lips, arms, legs, and some might use fingernails, teeth, or pins to scratch or pick (Wilhelm et al, 1999). Matsumoto et al. (2004) suggested arm cutting was related to anger expression but wrist cutting was not which implied the possible presence of subgroups even when the same method was adopted. Favazza (1998) classified NSSI into three groups, the major group referring to infrequent but severe act, the stereotypic group referring to rhythmic and repetitive self-mutilation like banging and hitting, the moderate group referring to episodic acts like cutting and compulsive acts like self-banging. Jacobson and Gould (2007) suggested frequency was related to functions of NSSI. Psychological correlates could also be classification criteria in subgroups, as psychological characteristics like anger and depression symptoms were identified as strongly related to NSSI.

*Gender Differences in Emotional Correlates and NSSI*

Though Patton et al (2007) alluded age of onset of NSSI was more related to puberty and the depressive symptoms resulted correspondingly in females. Females were found to have a later onset than males (Andover, Primack, Gibb, & Pepper, 2010), while some

suggested no gender difference on onset of NSSI (Gonzalez-Forteza et al, 2005).

Gender difference was identified in NSSI behaviors. O'Connoe, Rasmussen and Hawton

(2009) reported more females (65%) were present in the self-harmer group and in the repeater

group. Claes, Vandereycken, and Vertommen (2007) suggested self-injurious behavior was

1.5 to 3 times more likely in females compared to males. More females engaged in NSSI

(Patton, Hemphill, Beyers, Bond, Toubourou, McMorris, & Catalano, 2007; Jarvis, Ferrence,

Johnson, & Whitehead, 1976; Gonzalez-Forteza, Alvarez-Ruiz, Saldana-Hernandez, &

Carreno-Garcia, 2005).

While some suggested no gender difference on prevalence of NSSI, most agreed that

males used more violent methods (Bradvik, 2007). Claes et al (2007) found gender difference

in number and frequency of episodes, functions, feeling of negative emotions. More females

were identified in self-cutting and similar prevalence among methods other than cutting

(Andover et al, 2005). Claes et al (2007) found more cutting, scratching, bruising, and biting

among females while more burning was identified in males. Females were identified to have

more frequent NSSI (Laye-Gindhu & Schonert-Reichi, 2005). Females were more likely to

attempt suicide (Moscicki, 1994).

Previous studies focused on anger concluded different reasons on gender differences.

More males were identified as being in the high anger group (Gonzalez-Forteza et al, 2005;

Claes et al, 2007; Standford & Jones, 2009; Horesh, Gothelf, Ofek, Weizman, & Apter,

1999). Hawton, Rodham, Evans and Weatherall (2002) suggested no gender difference on the

degree of anger, while Horesh et al (1999) suggested more females showed self-aggression.

Such differences in findings were attributed to the different operational definitions of NSSI

and differences in type of NSSI investigated.

Compared to anger, gender difference on dysphoric mood and depressive symptoms

were less controversial. Rates of depression and most anxiety disorders were found to be

higher for females than males (Hasin, Goodwin, Stinson, & Grant, 2005). It was then

reasoned that more females had depressive symptoms and the group with more depressive

symptoms would have more females. Higher suicidal ideation/ attempt were found for

females, and females took more suicide attempts (Fortune & Hawton, 2005; Bradvik, 2007).

*Relations among Emotional Variables and NSSI*

<u>Anger</u>

Anger referred to an "emotional state that varies from mild irritation to intense rage",

and a common precursor to overt aggressive behaviors (Latalova & Prasko, 2010). Anger

could also be conceptualized as an emotional state that varied in intensity according to

situations, or as a trait with a relatively stable characteristic, and one might vary in the degree

of expressing or suppressing anger (Milligan & Waller, 2001). Anger resembled type A

personality with impulsivity and externalized anger as two main characteristics. Anger might be manifested in physical aggression like punching and pulling hair, in property destruction like tearing and breaking property, in stereotypic behavior like racking objects (Evenden, 1999).

Findings in the past in general suggested a higher prevalent rate of NSSI with more anger and more anger in individuals who performed NSSI. Carli et al (2010) suggested that individuals with higher aggression and hostility were highly impulsive and engaged more in self-mutilation, due to the failure in resisting the impulses to harm oneself physically. Self-injurers were more likely to practice aggressive behaviors (Claes et al, 2007). Anger was positively related to self-mutilation (Herpertz, Sass, & Favazza, 1997). Lutz et al (2002) also suggested a positive correlation among self-injury and externally directed aggression, but such correlation varied as a function of the social context. Degree of self-mutilation was significantly correlated with chronic anger (Simeon, Stanley, Frances, Mann, Winchel, & Stanley, 1992).

Self-injury was a kind of impulsive behavior that was self-directed. Some suggested such self-aggression behavior stemmed from redirected social aggression, individuals were unable to identify origins of frustration, hence directing aggression towards self in the form of self-injury (Jones & Daniels, 1996; Herpertz et al, 1997).

Anger was related to types of method. Degree of self-harm was correlated with anger and impulsivity (Simeon, Stanley, Frances, Mann, Winchel, & Stanley, 1992). The most common methods for high anger group self-injurers engaged more in hitting head, wrist

cutting and piercing the skin (Sakelliadis et al, 2009). Psychogenic excoriation was associated

with lack of anger-expressing ability, and directs such anger to self (Calikusu et al, 2002).

Dysphoric Mood

Dysphoric mood included common negative emotions like depression, anxiety and

tension or stress. Dysphoric mood were manifested as depressed feelings, feelings of

worthlessness and loss of interests. Findings from previous research in general suggested a

high correlation among depressive symptoms and NSSI. The study from Weissman (1974)

found that around 35 percent to 80 percent of self-harm group reported suffering from

depression. Ennis, Barnes, Kennedy, and Trachtenberg (1989) also found that about 80

percent of patients admitted deliberate self-harm were depressed to moderate or severe

degrees. Higher rate of self-mutilation was found in groups with more depressive symptoms,

and a large percentage (41.6%) internalizing depressive disorders diagnoses was reported in

adolescents engaging in NSSI (Andover et al, 2005; Tuisku, Pelkonen, Kiviruusu, Karlsson,

Ruuttu, & Marttunen, 2009; Standford & Jones, 2009). Though self-injurers were not all

diagnosed with depression, most showed at least moderate depression (Keuthan et al, 2000;

Nock & Mendes, 2008; Dyer et al, 2009).

Distress Tolerance

Distress tolerance was resistance towards negative emotions. Compared to anger and dysphoric mood, distress tolerance as psychological correlate was being less investigated in previous research. Nock and Mendes (2008) suggested self-injurers were less able to tolerate intense distress, and experiencing intolerable arousal when facing stressful events. Distress tolerance was related to NSSI as one performed NSSI to escape from intense emotional states (Favazza, 1996).

Emotional Reactivity

Emotional reactivity referred to the magnitude of response to an emotional stimulus (Glenn, Blumenthal, Klonsky, & Hajcak, 2011). Compared to anger and dysphoric mood, emotion reactivity as psychological correlate was being less investigated in previous research. Self-injury group was found to have more frequent and intense emotions and faced more difficulty in handling unpleasant emotions (Klonsky, Oltmanns, & Turkheimer, 2003; Nock, 2009; Gratz & Roemer, 2008; Heath, Toste, Nedecheva, & Charlebois, 2008). Glenn et al (2011) concluded more negative emotionality and greater interference from such emotional distress in the NSSI group. According to Nock (2009), intense negative emotional state preceded NSSI behaviors. Klonsky (2007) found that decrease in negative affect right after NSSI could predict lifetime frequency of that particular type of NSSI. Claes et al (2007) found that females had more intense emotions than males

*Relation between NSSI, Emotional Correlates and Suicide*

Some suggested that all self-harm behaviors lying on a continuum of lethality, while characteristics of deliberate self-harm was similar to complete suicide (Portzy & Heeringen, 2007). Frequency of suicide attempt was positively correlated with frequency, duration and number of methods of NSSI (Nock, Joiner Jr, Gordon, Lloyd-Richardson, & Prinstein, 2006). Stanley, Gaemeroff, Michalsen, and Mann (2001) also found more suicide attempt among self-injurers. Beautrais (2003) identified NSSI, males, depression as risk factors for suicide following self-harm.

Biochemical evidence was suggested to be the reason under the relations among anger, dysphoric mood, NSSI and suicide (Herpetz et al, 1997). Given the link among anger and sertonergic function, the study concluded that inwardly directed anger, depressive symptoms, NSSI, and suicide attempts presented a cohesive complex with a relative lack of sertonin.

Though relation between anger, dysphoric mood and suicidal attempt was affirmed, such relation might be confounded as self-injurers with high level of anger might choose more violent types of NSSI which harmed so much that death was caused unintentionally, whereas self-injurers with high dysphoric mood attempted more suicide even without NSSI. Van Orden, Merrill, and Joiner (2005) suggested that act of NSSI might habituate one to self-injury, which increased the risk of death by suicide.

*Purposes of the Present Study*

Previous research denoted that NSSI was common among adolescents, and different emotional variables, anger and dysphoric mood in particular, were highly correlated with

NSSI, whereas anger, dysphoric mood and NSSI were highly correlated with suicidal ideation and attempt. The present study examined emotional correlates of NSSI among Chinese adolescents in Hong Kong, and focused on two major aspects.

(1) Gender differences in emotional correlates and NSSI

(2) Relations among anger, dysphoric mood, suicidal ideation/attempt and NSSI

Chapter 2

METHOD

Participants and Procedure

Eight secondary schools in Hong Kong participated in the present study. Written

parental consent for student participation was obtained and the standard data collection

protocol was approved by the Ethics in Human Research Committee of the Chinese

University of Hong Kong. The questionnaires were completed in classrooms during a 45-

minute period. Students absent from school on the day of the study were later administered

questionnaires under the supervision of school personnel. Because of school authorities'

cooperation and strong encouragement of participation, overall student participation rates

were close to 99% in all schools. The present study included 5,422 adolescents (52.8%

females), aged between 13 and 21 years (M=14.60 years, SD=1.21).

*Measures*

Non-suicidal self-injury (NSSI)

Twelve types of NSSI behaviors were assessed in the study. Participants were asked "In

the past 12 months, have you ever intentionally, but not for suicide, 1) cut yourself; 2) burned

yourself; 3) carved words or pictures on the skin; 4) scratched skin thereby caused bleeding

or left scar; 5) inserted objects to the nail or skin; 6) pulled hair out; 7) bit yourself; 8) erase skin to draw blood; 9) eroded skin with acid; 10) scrubbed skin with bleach or cleaner; 11)

banged the head or other parts of the body against the wall; 12) punched yourself thereby

caused a bruise?". Each item was rated on a 4-point Likert scale, ranging from 1 "never", 2

"once or twice", 3 "three to five times", to 4 "six times or more". Summation of the 12 items

gives the total frequency of NSSI with various methods. These 12 items had a Cronbach's

alpha of .811 in the present study. Participants who endorsed one or more NSSI behaviors

would be instructed to state the age of onset of NSSI.

Dysphoric Mood

The Chinese version of the short Depression Anxiety Scale (DASS21; Taouk, Lovibond,

& Laube, 2001) was used to measure dysphoric moods. There were 21 items in this scale.

Sample items included "I feel that life was meaningless" and "I find it difficult to relax".

Responses were made on a 4-point Likert scale, ranging from 0 "do not apply to me at all" to

3, "apply to me very much or most of the time". Higher scores indicate more dysphoric

mood. This scale had a Cronbach's alpha of .933 in the present study.

Anger

Five items assessing aggressive impulse were extracted from the 12-items impulsive

behavior scale that was extracted and modified from the Diagnostic Interview of Borderlines

– Revised (DIB-R; Zanarini, Gunderson, Frankenburg, & Chauncey, 1989). Sample items

included "verbal outburst", "physical fights", "physical threats", "physical assaults" and "property damage". Participants rated the frequency of various impulsive behaviors displayed in the past one year and responses were made on a 4-point Likert scale, ranging from 1 "never", 2 "once or twice", 3 "three to five times" to 4 "6 times or more". Higher scores indicate more anger. The five items of anger had a Cronbach's alpha of .674 in the present study.

Distress Intolerance

The 15-item Distress Tolerance Scale (DTS; Simons & Gaher, 2005) was used to assess emotional distress tolerance. The DTS showed satisfactory internal consistency (satisfactory internal consistency ($\alpha$ = .89) and 6- week test-retest reliability ($r$ = .61) among college students. Participants rated how they felt when feeling suffering or in a bad mood on a 5-point Likert scale, ranging from 1 "strongly disagree" to 5 "strongly agree". Higher scores indicate more distress intolerance. Sample items included "Feeling distressed or upset is unbearable to me" and "I' ll do anything to avoid feeling distressed or upset". The scale had a Cronbach's alpha of .902 in the present study.

Emotional Reactivity

The 21-items Emotional Reactivity Scale (ERS; Nock, Wedig, Holmberg, & Hooley, 2008) was used to assess three areas of emotional reactivity, emotional sensitivity, emotional arousal or intensity, and emotion persistence. Participants rated how they experienced emotions on a regular basis on a 5-point Likert scale, ranging from 1 "strongly disagree" to 5 "strongly agree". Higher scores indicate more emotionally reactive. Sample items included "I tend to get emotional very easily", "I experience emotions very strongly" and "When I am angry or upset, it takes me longer than most people to calm down". The scale had a Cronbach's alpha of .961 in the present study.

Suicidal Ideation and Attempt

Suicidal ideation was measured by one item extracted from the depression subscale of the Depression Subscale of Symptoms Checklist-90 (SCL-90; Derogatis, Lipman & Covi, 1973). Participants rated how frequent they had the "thoughts of ending life" in the past one year on a 4-point Likert scale, ranging from 1 "never' to 4 "6 times or more". Suicidal attempt was measured by one item adapted from the Diagnostic Interview of Borderlines – Revised (DIB-R; Zanarini et al., 1989). Participants rated how frequent they attempted suicide in the past one year on a 4-point Likert scale, ranging from 1 "never" to 4 "6 times or more". Summation of the two items gave a composite score for subsequent analysis.

Demographics

Gender and age of the participants were also measured.

Chapter 3

RESULTS

*Sample Characteristics of all Participants in the Present Study*

Table 1 presents the means, standard deviations, Cronbach's alpha and the range of

score for all variables in the present study by gender. NSSI frequency was recoded and it

ranged from 0 "never", 1 "one or two times", 2 "three to five times" to 4 "six times or more).

Compared to males, females reported significantly higher levels of NSSI frequency, distress

intolerance, emotion reactivity, suicidal ideation and attempt, and a significantly later onset of

NSSI. Males reported significantly higher level of anger.

**Table 1**

*Sample Characteristics of All Participants ( N = 5423, 52.8% F, 47.2% M)*

| Variables | All Mean(SD) | F Mean(SD) | M Mean(SD) | t | p | α | Range |
|---|---|---|---|---|---|---|---|
| NSSI frequency | 1.07(2.63) | 1.20(2.72) | 0.91(2.50) | 3.944 | .000 | .811 | 0-36 |
| Age | 14.63(1.24) | 14.66(1.26) | 14.59(1.21) | 2.266 | .024 | | 12-19 |
| Age of onset | 10.64(3.06 | 11.17(2.50) | 9.83(3.60) | 6.670 | .000 | | 0-19 |
| Anger | 6.86(2.08) | 6.76(1.93) | 6.97(2.22) | -3.691 | .000 | .674 | 5-20 |
| Dysphoric mood | 13.84(11.42) | 13.94(11.07) | 13.72(11.77) | .682 | .495 | .933 | 0-63 |
| Distress intolerance | 38.72(11.37) | 39.95(10.63) | 37.31(11.97) | 8.372 | .000 | .902 | 15-75 |
| Emotion reactivity | 44.34(18.65) | 45.82(18.96) | 42.63(18.11) | 6.16 | .000 | .961 | 0-105 |
| Suicidal ideation and attempt | 2.25(0.69) | 2.30(0.74) | 2.20(0.62) | 5.902 | .000 | .467 | 2-8 |

A Chi-square analysis revealed significant gender difference in the prevalence of NSSI

(18.4% in female vs. 12.7% in males), $\chi^2 (1, N = 5423) = 38.983$, $p < .001$, denoting that

more females engaged in NSSI.

*Prevalence of 12 Types of NSSI among the Whole Sample*

Table 2 presents the prevalence of twelve types of NSSI with breakdown by using the

type of NSSI or not. Among the total sample, carving was the most prevalent type (19.8%), followed by pulling hair (10.5%), cutting (8.6%), biting (7.8%), scratching (6.7%), banging

(5.6%), inserting object (4.1%), punching (4.1%), erasing skin (3.0%), burning skin (1.6%),

bleaching (0.8%), and the least common type of NSSI was eroding skin (0.5%). When males

and females were compared separately, the five methods of NSSI with the highest frequency

in females were the same as the total sample, but the rank changed as cutting was the second

most prevalent method (6.2%) and pulling hair became the third (5.6%). For males, the rank

of the five highest frequency method were carving (7.8%), followed by pulling hair (4.9%),

biting (2.7%), punching (2.5%), and cutting (2.4%).

Significant gender differences were found in 7 out of 12 types of NSSI. More females

(6.2%) engaged in cutting than males (2.4%), $\chi^2$ (1, $N = 5316$) = 73.136, $p < .001$. More

females (12.0%) than males (7.8%) engaged in carving, $\chi^2(1, N = 5313)$ = 33.641, $p < .001$.

More females (4.4%) than males (2.3%) engaged in scratching, $\chi^2(1, N = 5314)$ = 27.083, $p$

$< .001$ Biting was more prevalent among females (5.0%) than males (2.7%), $\chi^2(1, N = 5312)$

= 25.971, $p < .001$. Males (0.4%) engaged more eroding skin than females (0.1%), $\chi^2(1, N =$

5313) = 9.858, $p < .01$. More males (0.5%) engaged in bleaching than females (0.3%), $\chi^2(1,$

$N = 5308)$ = 5.117, $p <.05$. Punching was more prevalent among males (2.5%) than females

(1.6%), $\chi^2(1, N = 5312)$ = 17.272, $p < .001$.

**Table 2**
*Percentage of All Participants Reporting Differenct Types of NSSI in the Past 12 Months ( N = 5423)*

| | Group | | | | | |
|---|---|---|---|---|---|---|
| | N | | | Y | | |
| | All | F | M | All | F | M |
| Cut | 91.4 | 46.6 | 44.9 | 8.6 | 6.2 | 2.4 |
| Burn | 98.4 | 52.1 | 46.3 | 1.6 | .7 | .7 |
| Carve | 80.2 | 40.7 | 39.5 | 19.8 | 12.0 | 7.8 |
| Scratch | 93.3 | 48.3 | 45.0 | 6.7 | 4.4 | 2.3 |
| Insert object | 95.9 | 50.3 | 45.6 | 4.1 | 2.4 | 1.7 |
| Pull hair | 8.95 | 47.1 | 42.4 | 10.5 | 5.6 | 4.9 |
| Bite | 92.2 | 47.7 | 44.5 | 7.8 | 5.0 | 2.7 |
| Erase skin | 97.0 | 51.0 | 46.0 | 3.0 | 1.8 | 1.3 |
| Erode skin | 99.5 | 52.7 | 46.9 | .5 | .1 | .4 |
| Bleach | 99.2 | 52.5 | 46.7 | .8 | .3 | .5 |
| Bang | 94.4 | 49.7 | 44.6 | 5.6 | 3.0 | 2.6 |
| Punch | 95.9 | 51.2 | 44.7 | 4.1 | 1.6 | 2.5 |

Note: Group N=Not using that NSSI method; Group Y=Have used that NSSI method (one time or more).

* significant at .05 level; ** significant at .01 level; *** significant at .001 level

*Correlations among Psychological Correlates and NSSI frequency*

Table 3 presents the correlation matrix among four psychological correlates, suicidal ideations and attempts, and NSSI frequency with breakdown by gender. Significant correlations were found among all variables. All four psychological correlates had significant correlations with NSSI frequency for both gender. Anger showed strong correlation with NSSI frequency for both females, $r(2856) = .365, p < .001$, and males, $r(2555) = .309, p < .001$. Dysphoric mood also showed strong correlations with NSSI frequency with for both females, $r(2856) = .407, p < .001$, and males, $r(2555) = .332, p < .001$. Emotion reactivity was significantly correlated with NSSI frequency for both females, $r(2856) = .351, p < .001$ and males, $r(2555) = .280, p < .001$. Distress intolerance was also significantly correlated with NSSI frequency, but with a lower strength.

Significant correlations were found among suicidal ideation and attempt and other variables. Strong correlations were found among suicidal scales and NSSI frequency on both

females, $r(2856) = .499, p < .001$, and males, $r(2555) = .352, p < .001$. Anger and suicidal

scales were significantly correlated in both females, $r(2856) = .335, p < .001$, and males,

$r(2555) = .297, p < .001$. Dysphoric mood also showed significant correlations with suicidal

ideation and attempt in both female, $r(2856) = .425, p < .001$, and males, $r(2555) = .312, p$

$< .001$. Both distress intolerance and emotion reactivity showed significant correlations with

suicidal ideation and attempt, but with a lower strength.

**Table 3**
*Correlations of NSSI and Psychological Variables of All Participant ( N = 5423, 52.8% F, 47.2% M)*

| | | | F | | | | |
|---|---|---|---|---|---|---|---|
| | | | | Psychological Correlates | | | |
| | | NSSI Freq | Anger | DASS | DTS | ERS | SUI |
| | NSSI Freq | 1 | .365(**) | .407(**) | .229(**) | .351(**) | .499(**) |
| | Anger | .309(**) | 1 | .358(**) | .222(**) | .355(**) | .335(**) |
| M | DASS | .332(**) | .340(**) | 1 | .498(**) | .700(**) | .425(**) |
| | DTS | .156(**) | .270(**) | .411(**) | 1 | .506(**) | .271(**) |
| | ERS | .280(**) | .361(**) | .695(**) | .470(**) | 1 | .337(**) |
| | SUI | .352(**) | .297(**) | .312(**) | .201(**) | .275(**) | 1 |

*Note:* NSSI Freq=frequency of NSSI; Anger=anger score; DASS=dysphoric mood; DTS=distress into
lerance; ERS=emotion reactivity; SUI=suicide ideation and attempt.
-. Correlation is significant at the 0.05 level (2-tailed). *. Correlation is significant at the 0.01 level (2-
tailed). **. Correlation is significant at the 0.001 level (2-tailed).

*Group Comparison by Cutting Severity*

Previous studies reported differences among occasional self-injurers from frequent self-

injurers. Cutting frequency was used in the present study to divide subjects into four

subgroups. It was chosen because cutting was reported as the most typical NSSI in previous

studies. Table 4 presents the results of the one-way ANOVA analysis for group comparison

with breakdown by cutting frequency. Means, standard deviations, F values and the p values were shown in Table 4.

It was found that groups with higher severity had higher scores on all four psychological

correlates, and suicidal ideation/attempt. Significant overall differences were found in anger,

$F(3, 5314) = 96.631, p < .001$; dysphoric mood, $F(3, 5314) = 122.10, p < .001$; distress

intolerance, $F(3, 5314) = 42.16, p < .001$; emotion reactivity, $F(3, 5314) = 108.52, p < .001$;

suicidal ideation/attempt, $F(3, 5314) = 346.791, p < .001$). No significant difference was

found in age of onset of NSSI.

Significant differences were found among group of no NSSI with all other three groups

on the various scales. Significant differences were also found among the mild NSSI group

with the moderate and severe groups. Among the moderate and severe groups, significant

differences were found in anger, and suicidal scales only.

**Table 4**
*Group Comparisons Using Cutting Severity (n= 5423)*

| | Control | Mild | Moderate | Severe | F | p |
|---|---|---|---|---|---|---|
| | (n= 4873) | (n= 319) | (n= 85) | (n= 53) | (df= 3) | |
| NSSI Frequency | 0.60(1.52)[a] | 4.44(3.72)[b] | 8.26(4.57)[c] | 12.66(8.00)[d] | 1389.26 | .000 |
| Age | 14.65(1.24)[a] | 14.64(1.14)[a] | 14.36(1.08)[a] | 14.38(1.32)[a] | 2.25 | .081 |
| Age of Onset | 10.44(3.19)[a] | 11.10(2.96)[a] | 10.88(2.53)[a] | 10.46(2.44)[a] | 2.88 | .035 |
| Anger | 6.73(1.95)[a] | 7.98(2.58)[b] | 8.46(2.55)[b] | 9.94(3.71)[c] | 96.63 | .000 |
| Dysphoric Mood | 12.96(10.78)[a] | 21.79(13.43)[b] | 26.53(13.71)[c] | 27.15(13.10)[c] | 122.10 | .000 |
| Distress Intolerance | 38.21(11.27)[a] | 43.66(10.58)[b] | 45.42(12.30)[b] | 47.71(11.65)[b] | 42.16 | .000 |
| Emotion Reactivity | 42.99(17.87)[a] | 56.91(20.53)[b] | 62.88(19.17)[c] | 65.30(22.66)[c] | 108.52 | .000 |
| Suicidal Idea and Act | 2.18(0.53)[a] | 2.80(1.13)[b] | 3.19(1.38)[c] | 4.33(1.96)[d] | 346.79 | .000 |

*Predicting NSSI Frequency Using Psychological Correlates among All Participants, Females*

*and Males*

Standard regression analysis were performed for the whole sample using NSSI frequency as dependent variable and anger, dysphoric mood, distress intolerance, and

emotion reactivity as independent variables. Table 5 presents the unstandardized regression

coefficients ($B$), the standardized regression coefficients ($\beta$), the semipartial correlations ($sr^2$),

$R$, $R^2$, and adjusted $R^2$. R for regression was significant for all samples, female and male

groups.

For the whole sample, $F(4, 4673) = 265.56$, $p < .001$. All predictors explained a total of

18.5% (18.5% adjusted) variances in NSSI frequency. Anger, dysphorc mood and emotion

reactivity were significant. Only anger and dysphoric mood made unique contribution in

predicting frequency of NSSI. Anger explained 4% and dysphoric mood explained 3% of the

unique variance in frequency of NSSI. All the four predictors in combination contributed

11.5% of shared variance in explaining the variance in NSSI frequency ($R^2$: .185 – the sum of

$sr^2$: .07 = .115). Explanatory power of anger and dysphoric mood were higher than distress

intolerance and emotion reactivity. Dysphoric mood ($\beta = .258$) was stronger than anger ($\beta =$

.206) in predicting the frequency of NSSI.

For females, $F(4, 2485) = 175.92$, $p < .001$. All predictors explained a total of 22.1%

(21.9% adjusted) variances in NSSI frequency. Only anger and dysphoric mood were

significant and making unique contribution in predicting frequency of NSSI. Anger explained

5.4% and dysphoric mood explained 4.7% of the unique variance in frequency of NSSI. All

the four predictors in combination contributed 11.8% of shared variance in explaining the variance in NSSI frequency ($R^2$: .219 – the sum of $sr^2$: .101= .118). Explanatory power of anger and dysphoric mood were higher than distress intolerance and emotion reactivity. Dysphoric mood ($\beta$ = .289) was stronger than anger ($\beta$ = .229) in predicting the frequency of NSSI.

For males, $F(4, 2169) = 102.95$, $p < .001$. All predictors explained a total of 16.0% (15.8% adjusted) variances in NSSI frequency. Only anger and dysphoric mood were significant and making unique contribution in predicting frequency of NSSI. Anger explained 3.5% and dysphoric mood explained 3.1% of the unique variance in frequency of NSSI. All the four predictors in combination contributed 9.3% of shared variance in explaining the variance in NSSI frequency ($R^2$: .160 – the sum of $sr^2$: .066= .094). Explanatory power of anger and dysphoric mood were higher than distress intolerance and emotion reactivity. Dysphoric mood ($\beta$ = .251) was stronger than anger ($\beta$ = .204) in predicting the frequency of NSSI.

**Table 5**

*Standard Regression Analysis Using Psychological Correlates Predicting NSSI Frequency in All Participants, Female and Male (All: N=5423, F(4,4673) = 265.557, p < .001; Female: N=2856, F(4, 2485) = 175.92, p < .001; Male: N=2555, F(4, 2169) = 102.95, p < .001)*

| Predictors | All | | | F | | | M | | |
|---|---|---|---|---|---|---|---|---|---|
| | $B$ | $\beta$ | $sr^2$ | $B$ | $\beta$ | $sr^2$ | $B$ | $\beta$ | $sr^2$ |
| Anger | .507*** | .206 | .04 | .653*** | .229 | .054 | .422 | .204 | .035 |
| DYS | .631*** | .258 | .03 | .781*** | .289 | .047 | .536 | .251 | .031 |
| DTS | -.014 | -.006 | .00 | -.030 | -.011 | .00 | -.044*** | -.021 | .00 |
| EMO | .173*** | .070 | .00 | .170 | .066 | .00 | .108*** | .048 | .00 |
| | | | $R = .430$*** | | | $R = .470$*** | | | $R = .423$*** |
| | | | $R^2 = .185$ | | | $R^2 = .221$ | | | $R^2 = .179$ |
| | | | Adjusted $R^2 = .185$ | | | Adjusted $R^2 = .219$ | | | Adjusted $R^2 = .177$ |
| | | | Shared variance = .115 | | | Shared variance = .118 | | | Shared variance = .118 |

*Note.* DYS=Dysphoric mood; DTS=Distress intolerance; EMO=Emotion Reactivity.
* significant at .05 level; ** significant at .01 level; *** significant at .001 level

*Predicting Suicidal Ideation and Attempt Using Psychological Correlates and NSSI among*

*All Participants, Females and Males*

Standard regression analysis were performed for the whole sample, females and males

using suicidal ideation and attempt as dependent variable and anger, dysphoric mood, distress

intolerance, emotion reactivity, and NSSI frequency as independent variables. Table 6

presents the unstandardized regression coefficients ($B$), the standardized regression

coefficients ($\beta$), the semipartial correlations ($sr^2$), $R$, $R^2$, and adjusted $R^2$. R for regression was

significant for the whole sample, female and male groups

For all participant, $F(5, 4670) = 330.148$, $p < .001$. All predictors explained a total of

26.1% (26.0% adjusted) variances in suicidal ideation and attempt. Anger, dysphorc mood,

distress intolerance and NSSI frequency were significant. Only anger, dysphoric mood and

NSSI frequency made unique contribution in predicting suicidal ideation and attempt. NSSI

frequency explained 7.7% of the unique variance in suicidal ideation and attempt. Anger

explained only 1.4% and dysphoric mood explained only 1.4% of the unique variance in

suicidal ideation and attempt. All the four predictors in combination contributed 15.6% of

shared variance in explaining the variance in NSSI frequency ($R^2$: .261 – the sum of $sr^2$: .105

= .156). Explanatory power of NSSI frequency was the highest ($\beta = .307$), and anger and

dysphoric mood were higher than distress intolerance and emotion reactivity. Dysphoric

mood ($\beta = .177$) was stronger than anger ($\beta = .130$) in predicting the frequency of NSSI.

For females, $F(5, 2483) = 243.14$, $p < .001$. All predictors explained a total of 32.9%

(32.7% adjusted) variances in suicidal ideation and attempt. Anger, dysphoric mood, distress

intolerance and NSSI frequency were significant. Only anger, dysphoric mood and NSSI

frequency made unique contribution in predicting suicidal ideation and attempt. NSSI

frequency explained 10.4% of the unique variance in suicidal ideation and attempt. Anger

explained only 1.1% and dysphoric mood explained only 2.2% of the unique variance in

suicidal ideation and attempt. All the four predictors in combination contributed 19.2% of

shared variance in explaining the variance in NSSI frequency ($R^2$: .329 – the sum of $sr^2$: .137

= .192). Explanatory power of NSSI frequency was the highest ($\beta = .365$), and anger and

dysphoric mood were higher than distress intolerance and emotion reactivity. Dysphoric

mood ($\beta = .221$) was stronger than anger ($\beta = .116$) in predicting the frequency of NSSI.

For males, $F(5, 2167) = 94.71$, $p < .001$. All predictors explained a total of 17.9%

(17.7% adjusted) variances in suicidal ideation and attempt. Anger, dysphoric mood, distress

intolerance and NSSI frequency were significant. Only anger, dysphoric mood and NSSI

frequency made unique contribution in predicting suicidal ideation and attempt. NSSI

frequency explained 3.5% of the unique variance in suicidal ideation and attempt. Anger

explained only 2.3% and dysphoric mood explained only 0.9% of the unique variance in

suicidal ideation and attempt. All the four predictors in combination contributed 11.8% of

shared variance in explaining the variance in NSSI frequency ($R^2$: .179 – the sum of $sr^2$: .067

= .118). Explanatory power of NSSI frequency was the highest ($\beta$ = .202), and anger and

dysphoric mood were higher than distress intolerance and emotion reactivity. Anger ($\beta$ = .

169) was stronger than dysphoric mood ($\beta$ = .141) in predicting the frequency of NSSI.

**Table 6**

*Standard Regression Analysis Using Psychological Correlates and NSSI Frequency Predicting Suicidal Ideation and Attempt in All Participant, Female and Male (All: N=5423, F(5,4670) = 330.148, p < .001; Female: N=2856, F(5, 2483) = 243.14, p < .001; Male: N=2555, F(5, 2167) = 94.71, p < .001)*

| Predictors | All | | | F | | | M | | |
|---|---|---|---|---|---|---|---|---|---|
| | $B$ | $\beta$ | $sr^2$ | $B$ | $\beta$ | $sr^2$ | $B$ | $\beta$ | $sr^2$ |
| Anger | .090*** | .130 | .014 | .092*** | .116 | .011 | .098*** | .169 | .023 |
| DYS | .121*** | .177 | .014 | .166*** | .221 | .022 | .085*** | .141 | .009 |
| DTS | .040*** | .058 | .00 | .046** | .058 | .00 | .026* | .045 | .00 |
| EMO | .015 | .021 | .00 | -.011 | -.015 | .00 | .023 | .036 | .00 |
| Freq | .226*** | .307 | .077 | .267*** | .365 | .104 | .150*** | .202 | .035 |
| | $R$ =.511*** | | | $R$ =.573*** | | | $R$ =.423*** | | |
| | $R^2$ = .261 | | | $R^2$ = .329 | | | $R^2$ = .179 | | |
| | Adjusted $R^2$ = .260 | | | Adjusted $R^2$ = .327 | | | Adjusted $R^2$ = .177 | | |
| | Shared variance = .156 | | | Shared variance = .192 | | | Shared variance = .118 | | |

*Note.* DYS=Dysphoric mood; DTS=Distress intolerance; EMO=Emotion Reactivity; Freq=NSSI frequency.
* significant at .05 level; ** significant at .01 level; *** significant at .001 level

Chapter 4

DISCUSSION

The present study examines the emotional correlates of NSSI among Chinese

adolescents in Hong Kong. There were two primary objectives in present study. We first

investigated gender differences in emotional correlates and NSSI. Relations among anger,

dysphoric mood, suicidal ideation/ attempt and NSSI frequency of NSSI were also examined.

*Gender differences in Emotional Correlates and NSSI*

Females reported higher frequency of NSSI in present study. Result was in accordance

with plentiful research indicating higher prevalence of NSSI in females (O'Connor et al,

2009; Claes et al, 2006; Patton et al, 2007; Jarvis et al, 2010). One possible explanation might

have to do with the inclusive criteria of NSSI. Males engaged more in risk-taking behaviors

which were not included in NSSI. Gender differences in the prevalence of NSSI might reflect

the use of different pathological form of coping strategies to deal with negative emotion

(Ross & Heath, 2002). Another possible explanation might have to do with the acceptability

of expressing anger outwardly. Herpretz et al (1997) suggested that NSSI related more to

anger directed inwards than outwards. With lower acceptability in expressing anger

outwardly, females directed frustration towards self through NSSI, the typical gender pattern

in NSSI was resulted (Bennum, 1983; Fazavva, 1998).

The later onset of NSSI reported by females was consistent with a previous finding

(Gonzalez-Forteza et al, 2005). Females reported more distress intolerance and emotion reactivity. This finding was also consistent with previous research which indicated more intense emotions in females (Claes et al, 2006). Higher level of anger reported by males was also in accordance with plentiful research reporting higher anger level among males (Gonzalez-Forteza et al, 2005; Claes et al, 2006). In contrast, no gender difference was found on dysphoric mood. This finding contradicted with previous research that more depressive symptoms and rate of depression were higher among females (Hilt, Cha, & Nolen-Hoeksema, 2008). One might use NSSI as a mean to regulate negative emotions, but one might also be distressed by the engagement in NSSI behaviors. Lochner et al (2002) suggested self-injurers engaging in skin picking were distressed by not able to control the impulse to engage in NSSI. Dysphoric mood could be a trait, a relatively stable characteristic, or state, which varied in intensity and being experienced continuously or in episodes. Though females were prone to depressive symptoms, males were possible to feel high level of dysphoric mood as states. Females also reported more suicidal ideation and attempt, which matched with previous findings (Bradvik, 2007).

*Gender Differences on Types on NSSI*

Findings of present study denoted 31.1% (18.4% of females and 12.7% of males) of adolescents engaged in one of more types of NSSI in the past 12 months. The prevalence rate was much higher than the rate (3.8%) obtained in another study in Hong Kong (Wong,

Stewart, Ho, & Lam, 2007). One possible explanation might have to do with the inclusion of

more types of NSSI. Compared the study of Wong et al (2007), present study included 12

types of NSSI, which possibly include more self-injurers. Another possible explanation might

have to do with ambiguous wordings of NSSI methods and inadequate understandings among

adolescents on NSSI. Carving (19.8%), pulling hair (20.5%), cutting (8.6%), biting (7.8%)

and scratching (6.7%) were the five most common methods of NSSI in present study. Orders

of the top five prevalent NSSI methods were different across genders. For females, carving

(12.0%) was the most prevalent one, followed by cutting (6.2%), pulling hair (5.6%), biting

(5.0%) and scratching (4.4%). Other seven types of NSSI had prevalent rate from 0.1% to

3.0%. For males, carving (7.8%) was the most prevalent one, followed by pulling hair

(4.9%), biting (2.7%), punching (2.5%) and cutting (2.4%). Other seven types of NSSI had

prevalent rate from 0.4% to 2.3%. Findings from this study were quite a few varied from

findings in previous research suggesting cutting, burning, biting, punching and banging were

the most five common types of NSSI, though one study from Nock and Prinstein (2004)

suggested cutting or carving was one of the most common method. In present study, only

cutting and biting remained in the top five ranking of NSSI methods in both genders. Rate of

banging was 3.0% in females and 2.6% in males, and rate of punching was 1.6% in females

and 2.5% of males. Rate of burning was 0.7% in both genders. These discrepancies might be

possibly explained by ambiguous terms of NSSI. Participants might misunderstand the methods of NSSI, mistakenly regarded the non-NSSI scratching, biting or pulling hair as methods of NSSI, or they might mistakenly equalized carving with cutting. These resulted in more report of having NSSI, especially on the non-typical methods of NSSI.

Prevalence of cutting and biting were higher in females, while males had higher prevalence of punching. Claes et al (2007) suggested females engaged in NSSI for emotion regulation, and released negative emotions and frustrations towards self through acting-in NSSI methods that hurt directly, like cutting and biting. Thus females showed significantly more "relieved" emotion right after NSSI (Claes et al, 2007). Rate of punching among gender was consistent with some previous research. Males showed more outwardly directed anger and impulse to express frustration in a way that influenced others, so they engaged more in acting-out NSSI methods like punching (Cheng & Mallinckrodt, 2010). Following this explanation, males should also show higher prevalence in banging, but prevalence of banging across gender was comparable in the present study (3.0% in females vs. 2.6% in males). One possible explanation might have to do with the inclusive criteria of banging. Claes et al (2007) and Sakelliadis et al (2009) found that more males engaged in head banging, while banging in present study included banging of head and other body parts, we could not rule out the possibility that males still showed more head banging.

Another possible explanation might have to do with functions in engaging banging and punching (Ross & Heath, 2002; Jones & Daniels, 1996; Herpertz et al, 1997). Banging was a mean to express anger to others, as self-injurers reported an inability to hit others and so

directing anger onto objects. Self-punching was a mean to represent self-hatred and a wish to

punish oneself. In the present study, no gender difference was found on dysphoric mood.

Dysphoric mood was comparable to anger acting inwards. According this explanation, more

males should used banging while more females should used punching, but such trends were

reversed in present study. One possible explanation might have to do with the use of three

subscales, depression, anxiety, tension/distress to represent dysphoric mood. Another possible

explanation was that females had more difficulty in expressing anger and thus redirect anger

to self through other methods like cutting, while cutting was not common in males due to the

"feminine" nature. Males might use more aggressive methods like punching for the same

function (Soloff, Lis, Kelly, Cornelius, & Ulrich, 1994).

Though males showed higher level of outwardly directed anger, we could not rule out

the possibility that males had expressed that anger towards people who angered them.

Together with the lower acceptability of females to express outwardly-directed anger, females

were more likely to direct unexpressed anger to objects like wall, which resulted in the

pattern of banging (3.0% in females vs. 2.6% in males) and punching (1.6% in females vs.

2.5% in males) in present study. Findings on pulling hair (5.6% in females vs. 4.9% in males)

were consistent with the result from Keuthen et al (2002), suggesting that more depressed

individuals used more hair-pulling. As females showed a little higher level in dysphoric mood, prevalence of pulling hair showed similar trend compared to dysphoric mood, with a

little higher prevalence in females, though difference in prevalence was not significant. The

comparable results from two genders on dysphoric mood and punching might imply a similar

level of dysphoric mood across genders, and resulted in similar prevalence in methods like

punching.

*Correlations among NSSI, Emotional Variables and Suicidal Ideation and Attempt among*

*Females and Males*

Frequency of NSSI was positively related to all other variables in present study. For

females, the magnitude of correlations with psychological correlates ranged from .229 to .

407, and .499 with suicidal ideation and attempt. For males, the magnitude of correlations

with psychological correlates ranged from .156 to .332, and .352 with suicidal ideation and

attempt. The findings in the present study were consistent with previous research that NSSI

was positively correlated with anger (Carli et al, 2010; Claes et al, 2006; Herpertz et al,

1997), dysphoric mood (Andover et al, 2005; Tuisku et al, 2009), distress intolerance (Nock

& Mendes, 2008), emotion reactivity (Glenn et al, 2011), and suicidal ideation/ attempt

(Stanley et al, 2001).

Suicidal ideation/ attempt were also positively correlated with anger and dysphoric

mood across genders. For females, the magnitude of the correlation was .335 with anger

and .425 with dysphoric mood. For males, the magnitude of correlation was .297 with anger and .312 with dysphoric mood. Findings were consistent with previous research suggesting a

positive correlation among anger and NSSI (Stanley et al, 2001; Nock & Marzuik, 2000), a

positive correlation among dysphoric mood and NSSI (Brent, 1993; Kim, Lesage, Seguin,

Lipp, Vanier, & Tureki, 2003).

*Subgroups of NSSI: Cutting Severity*

Most previous research studied self-injurers as a homogeneous group and had not

verified variances among self-injurers. Previous study proposed various ways to classify self-

injurers (Kumar et al, 2004). Present study classified subgroups of self-injurers based on the

severity of cutting behavior. Cutting was used for comparison as it was identified as the most

typical NSSI method, though this was not shown in our findings. Severity was based on the

frequency of cutting, self-injurers with one to two times of cut in the past 12 months were

likely to be an episodic subgroup, while self-injurers with three to five times, six times or

more cut were likely to be a repetitive subgroup. Findings in the present study indicated

lower level of psychological correlates and suicidal ideation/ attempt in non-cutting

subgroup. This was consistent with previous research suggesting correlations among NSSI

with psychological correlates, and suicidal ideation/ attempt, signifying higher anger and

dysphoric mood, lower ability to tolerate distress, more emotion reactive and more suicidal

ideation/ attempt. With intense negative emotions, one might engage NSSI for functions like

emotion regulation and anger expression.

In present study, it was observed that severe cutting subgroup had highest level in all variables, followed by second highest level in moderate, mild, and non-cutting subgroup. Distress intolerance level was comparable among the three cutting subgroups, with significant differences among mild and severe groups. The moderate and severe groups only differed in NSSI frequency, anger and suicidal ideation/ attempt, implying that the two groups were comparable. Mild self-cutters, who were likely to be episodic self-cutters, showed lower levels in NSSI frequency, dysphoric mood, emotion reactivity and suicidal ideation/ attempt compared to moderate and severe groups, while differences in anger and distress intolerance were only differed from severe group.

These suggested the repetitive subgroup, including moderate and severe self-cutters, experienced more emotional disturbances than mild cutters and non-cutting groups. One possible explanation might be that moderate and severe self-cutters possessed certain relatively stable traits in predisposing them to NSSI, while mild cutters used NSSI in states. With originally more disturbances in psychological correlates, and provided with relieved feelings or perceptions of ability to tolerate stress after NSSI, they might learn through negative reinforcement to use more NSSI as maladaptive strategies to cope with stress (Suyemoto & Macdonald, 1995). This was consistent with the positive correlations among psychological correlates and NSSI frequency. The positive correlation implied another possible explanation. One might feel distressed because of the inability to control or stop

NSSI behaviors (Lochner et al, 2002). With higher frequency of NSSI, one might feel more

disturbed because of the inability to control the impulse to engage in NSSI, resulting in

higher levels of negative emotions and emotional disturbances in moderate and severe self-

cutters. The seriously disturbed emotions of repetitive self-cutters might effectively be

regulated by NSSI, but not for the mild self-cutters. Mild self-cutters might not need frequent

NSSI due to lower levels of emotional disturbances and suicidal ideation/ attempt.

*Relative Importance of Anger and Dysphoric Mood in Predicting Frequency of NSSI*

Regression analysis all psychological correlates together explained a moderate amount

of variance in NSSI frequency (18.5% in whole sample, 22.1% in females and 17.9% in

males). Dysphoric mood was the strongest predictors of NSSI frequency among four

psychological correlates ($\beta$ = .258 in the whole sample, $\beta$ = .289 in females and $\beta$ = .251 in

males) when relationships among predictors were not considered. All four psychological

correlates showed a shared variance of 11.5%. With considering the shared variances among

predictors, anger gave highest unique variance among the four (4% in the whole sample,

5.4% in females and 3.5% in males), followed by dysphoric mood (3% in the whole sample,

4.7% in females and 3.1% in males), while both distress intolerance and emotional reactivity

gave zero unique variance. Anger and dysphoric mood better explained the variance in NSSI

frequency in females than males. Though two predictors explained variances in NSSI

frequency, the unique effects of them were small, which suggested that anger and dysphoric mood did not have considerable predicting effect on NSSI frequency when relationships with other predictors were taken out. This also suggested the importance of considering the psychological correlates as a matrix and took relationships among psychological correlates into account in predicting NSSI.

One possible explanation might have to do with the strong correlations among psychological correlates in the present study. Positive correlations ranging from .222 to .700 in females, and from .261 to .695 in males were found among the four psychological correlates. Anger was correlated with dysphoric mood (.358 in females and .340 in anger) and emotion reactivity (.355 in females and .361 in males); dysphoric mood was correlated with distress intolerance (.498 in females and .411 in males); emotion reactivity was correlated with dysphoric mood (.700 in females and .695 in males) and distress intolerance (.506 in females and .470 in males). Though predictors like emotional reactivity and distress intolerance showed no unique effect in explaining the variances in NSSI frequency, they might effect through relationships with other psychological correlates. Anger and dysphoric mood might also effect through the relationships with other correlates, besides the unique contributions in predicting NSSI frequency. Previous study also suggested a possible relationship among anger and dysphoric mood, and possible moderating or mediating effects by other psychological correlates (Stanley et al, 2010). Importance of considering the NSSI, psychological correlates and suicidal ideation and attempt as a complex matrix in explaining the NSSI and suicidal phenomenon was also suggested (Carli et al, 2010). Another possible

explanation might have to do with the psychological correlates chosen in present study. High

level of impulsivity was considered as an important psychological correlate in NSSI (Horesh

et al, 1999; Simeon et al, 1992; Stanley et al, 2001; Carli et al, 2010; Standford and Jone,

2009). Impulsivity was conceptualized as "behaving without considering the risk involved in

behaviors that might have undesirable consequences" (Parker, Bagby, & Webster, 1993;

Daruna & Barnes, 1993). Though anger seemed like impulsivity, it was found that individuals

engaging in impulsive behaviors could have extreme levels of anger, while a positive

correlation of .61 was still found among (Milligan & Waller, 2001; Simeon et al, 1992). NSSI

behavior was considered as a kind of impulsive behavior, implying a strong correlation

among impulsivity and NSSI. With the exclusion of impulsivity, overall explanatory power of

psychological correlates in the present study might be lessened. Our findings indicated

possible predicting powers of anger and dysphoric mood on NSSI frequency. Further

exploration on the potential interaction among psychological correlates in explaining NSSI,

and investigating extra possible predictors on NSSI frequency might provide further insights

on the effects of psychological correlates on NSSI.

*Relative Importance of NSSI Frequency, Anger and Dysphoric Mood in Predicting Suicidal*

*Ideation and Attempt*

Regression analysis showed that NSSI frequency and four psychological correlates together explained a moderate amount of the variance in suicidal ideation/ attempt, especially

for females (26.1% in the whole sample, 32.9% in females and 17.9% in males). Without

considering the relationship among predictors, NSSI frequency was the strongest predictor

for suicidal ideation/ attempt ($\beta$ = .307 in the whole sample, $\beta$ = .365 in females, and $\beta$ = .202

in males). Dysphoric mood was the second strongest predictor in the whole sample ($\beta$ = .177)

and females ($\beta$ = .221), while anger was the second strongest predictor for males ($\beta$ = .169),

with very small predicting effect from distress intolerance and emotion reactivity.

After considering relationship among predictors, NSSI frequency was still the strongest

predictor among the five, with a unique variance of 7.7% in the whole sample, 10.4% in

females, and 3.5% in males. This clearly indicated the importance of NSSI frequency in

predicting suicidal phenomenon. Importance of NSSI frequency on suicidal ideation/ attempt

was consistent with previous research suggesting co-occurrence or correlation among them

(Brown, Comtois, & Linehan, 2002; Beauratis, 2003). Findings in present study indicated

that NSSI frequency was more important in predicting suicidal ideation/ attempt in females,

but such importance was not so significant in males.

Both anger and dysphoric mood showed 1.4% of unique variance in the whole sample.

In females, dysphoric mood and anger showed 2.21% and 1.1% of unique variance in

predicting suicidal ideation/ attempt, indicating that dysphoric mood better explained the

suicidal ideation/ attempt in females. In males, dysphoric mood and anger showed 0.9% and

2.3% of unique variance in predicting suicidal ideation/ attempt, indicating that anger

provided better predictability in males. This was consistent with previous findings that there

was a positive correlation among anger, impulsivity and suicidal phenomenon, and the trend

was more significant in males (Horesh et al, 1999). The findings that dysphoric mood better

explained or equally explained suicidal phenomenon contradicted with previous findings that

self-mutilating suicide attempters showed more aggressiveness and together with impulsivity,

they were factors that mostly distinguished and explained suicidal ideation/ attempt (Stanley

et al, 2001; Nock & Marzuk, 2000). Portzky and Heeringen (2007) found higher suicidal

ideation/ attempt in adolescents with depressive symptoms, but as females and males showed

no significant difference in dysphoric mood, the explanatory difference of dysphoric mood on

suicidal ideation/ attempt across genders could not be addressed by this.

Though NSSI frequency and four psychological correlates explained moderate amount

of variances in suicidal phenomenon, most of the explanatory effect went to the shared

variance among predictors (15.6% in the whole sample, 19.2% in females, and 11.8% in

males). The unique predicting abilities of anger and dysphoric mood were small, indicating

that their individual effects in predicting suicidal ideation/ attempt were not so important,

while their effects were larger when they were considered together with other psychological

correlates. Similar explanations for the predicting ability of psychological correlates on NSSI

frequency might also be possible for explaining the small predicting ability of psychological correlates on suicidal ideation/ attempt. Predicting ability of predictors might effect through the correlations with other predictors, and the unique predicting ability might also be moderated or mediated by other factors. Horesh et al, (1999) suggested correlates like impulsivity had strong correlation with NSSI frequency and suicidal phenomenon, but such correlate was not included in present study.

Another possible reason might have to do with the direction of prediction. Although both present and previous studies suggested significant differences were found in psychological correlates, NSSI frequency and suicidal phenomenon among self-injurers and non self-injurers, significant differences among these variables could be causes, effects, or there might be bi-directional relationships among the psychological correlates, NSSI frequency and suicidal ideation/ attempt. Our findings indicated possible predicting powers of anger, dysphoric mood and NSSI frequency on suidality. Further exploration on the potential interaction among psychological correlates and the direction of predictions, might provide further insights on explaining NSSI prevalence with psychological correlates.

*Strengths and Limitations of the Present Study and Future Directions*

There are several strengths in the present study. First, the large sample size in our study increases the reliability and enriches the meaningfulness in interpreting our findings. Second, well-established scales with enough items ensures the reliability of the findings as well.

Some limitations in the present study should also be remarked. First, the study was done based on self-report questionnaires, and some might not provide answers according to actual situations. Self-report measures limit the depth of study; in-depth information concerning NSSI might be identified through other data-collection methods like interviews. Also, adolescents' misunderstandings on the wordings of items could not be answered, and the results might just different from real situations. Second, though the sample size was large, it still may not be able to represent the NSSI phenomenon in Hong Kong. There are still possibilities that certain schools might contain more self-injurers than others. It is helpful for future research to consider the NSSI prevalence among schools when conducting prevalence study again. Third, several psychological correlates, like anger, were measured with a few items only, and this might not account the whole picture in the correlates. It is helpful for future research to use more scales in measuring psychological correlates so as to improve the reliability of findings.

*Clinical Implications*

Despite of the limitations, findings of the present study have some important clinical implications. First, phenomenon of NSSI is relatively common among adolescents in Hong Kong. Around 31.1% of the participants in present study reported history of NSSI in the past 12 months, yet the prevalence may already be lessened as self-injurers who ceased NSSI before one year were not included in the group with NSSI. Given that NSSI and the underlying emotion disturbances may affect one's functioning, it is important for clinicians to pay careful attention to identify any possible signs of NSSI among adolescents, so as to

provide earlier intervention. Schools and families should also pay more attention to this issue

and provide more support to adolescents. The community as a whole should work together to

provide better and coherent intervention to confront NSSI behaviors among adolescents.

Reference

Andover, M. S., Pepper, C. M., Ryavchenko, K. A., Orrico, E. G., & Gibb, B. E. (2005).

Self-mutilation and symptoms of depression, anxiety, and borderline  personality

disorder. *Suicide & Life-Threatening Behavior, 35*(5), 581-591.

Andover, M. S., Primack, J. M., Gibb, B. E., & Pepper, C. M. (2010). An examination of

non-suicidal self-injury in men: Do men differ from women in basic NSSI

characteristics?. *Archives of Suicide Research, 14*, 79-88.

Beautrais, A. L. (2003). Subsequent mortality in medically serious suicide attempts.

*Australian and New Zealand Journal of Psychiatry, 37*, 595-599.

Bennum, I. (1983). Depression and hostility in self-mutilation. *Suicide Life Threat Behavior,*

*13*, 71-84.

Bradvik, L. (2007). Violent and nonviolent methods of suicide: Different patterns may be

found in men and women with severe depression. *Archives of Suicide Research, 11*,

255-264.

Brent, D. A. (1993). Depression and suicide in children and adolescents. *Pediatrics in*

*Review, 14*, 380-388.

Briere, J., & Gil, E. (1998). Self-mutilation in clinical and general population samples:

Prevalence, correlates, and functions. *American Journal of Orthopsychiatry, 68*,

609–620.

Brown, S. A., Williams, K., & Collins, A. (2007). Past and recent self-harm: Emotion and

coping strategy differences. *Journal of Clinical Psychology, 63*(9), 791-803.

Brown, M. Z., Comtios, K. A., & Linehan, M. M. (2002). Reasons for suicide attempts and

nonsuicidal self-injury in women with borderline personality disorder. *Journal of*

*Abnormal Psychology, 111*, 198-202.

Calikusu, C., Yucel, B., Polat., A., & Baykal, C. (2002). Expression of anger and alexithymia

in patients with psychogenic excoriation: A preliminary report. *International Journal*

*of Psychiatry in Medicine, 32*(4), 345-352.

Carli, V., Jovanovic, N., Podlesek, A., Roy, A., Rihmer, Z., Maggi, S., Marusic, D., Cesaro,

C., Marusic, A., & Sarchiapone, M. ( 2010). The role of impulsivity in self-mutilators,

suicide ideators and suicide attempters- A study of 1265 male incarcerated individuals.

*Journal of Affective Disorders, 123*, 116-122.

Cheng, H. L., & Mallinckrodt, B. (2010). Developing a screening instrument and at-risk

profile for nonsuicidal self-injurious behavior in college women and men. *Journal of*

*Counseling Psychology, 57*(1), 128-139.

Claes, L., Vandereycken, W., & Vertommen, H. (2007). Self-injury in female versus male

psychiatric patients: A comparison of characteristics, psychopathology and aggression

regulation. *Personality and Individual Differences, 42*, 611-621.

Daruna, J. H., & Barnes, P. A. (1993). A neurodevelopmental view of impulsivity. In W. G.

McCown, J. L. Johnson, & M. B. Shure (Eds.), *The impulsive client: Theory, research, and treatment* (pp. 23–37). Washington, DC: American Psychological Association.

Dyer, K. F. W., Dorahy, M. J., Hamilton, G., Corry, M., Shannon, M., MacSherry, A., McRobert, G., & Elder, R. (2009). Anger, aggression, and self-harm in PTSD and complex PTSD. *Journal of clinical Psychology, 65*(10), 1099-1114.

Ennis, J., Barnes, R. A., Kennedy, S., & Trachtenberg, D. D. (1989). Depression in self-harm patients. *British Journal of Psychiatry, 154*,41-47.

Evenden, J. L. (1999). Varieties of impulsivity. *Psychopharmacology, 146*, 348-361.

Favazza, A. R. (1998). The coming of age of self-mutilation. *Journal of Nervous and Mental Disease, 186*, 259-268.

Favazza, A. R. (1996). *Bodies under siege: Self-mutilation and body modification in culture and psychiatry (2nd ed.).* Baltimore: Johns Hopkins University Press.

Fortune, S. A., & Hawton, K. (2005). Deliberate self-harm in children and adolescents: A research update. *Current Opinion in Psychiatry, 18*, 401-406.

Glenn, C. R., Blumenthal, T. D., Klonsky, E.D., & Hajcak, G. (in press). Emotional reactivity in nonsuicidal self-injury: Divergence between self-report and startle measures. *International Journal of Psychophysiology.*

Gonzalez-Forteza, C., Alvarez-Ruiz, M., Saldana-Hernandez, A., Carreno-Garcia, S., Chavez-Hernandez, M., & Perez-Hernadez, R. (2005). Prevalence of deliberate self-harm in teenage students in the state of Guanajuato, Mexico:2003. *Social Behavior and*

*Personality, 33*(8), 777-791.

Gratz, K.L., Roemer, L., 2008. The relationship between emotion dysregulation and

deliberate self-harm among female undergraduate students at an urban commuter

university. *Cognitive Behavior Therapy, 37*, 14-25.

Greg Carter, D. M., Reith, I. M., Whyte, M. M. (2005). Non-suicidal deaths following

hospital-treated self-poisoning. *Australian and New Zealand Journal of Psychiatry,*

*39*(1), 101-107.

Hasin, D. S., Goodwin, R. D., Stinson, F. S., & Grant, B. F. (2005). Epidemiology of major

depressive disorder: Results from the national epidemiologic survey on alcoholism and

related conditions. *Archives of General Psychiatry, 65*, 1097-1106.

Hawton, K., & Fagg, J. (1992). Deliberate self-poisoning in adolescents: A study of

characteristics and trends in Oxford, 1976-89. *British Journal of Psychiatry, 161*,

816-823.

Hawton, K., Rodham, K., Evans, E., & Weatherall, R. (2002). Deliberate self harm in

adolescents: Self-report survey in schools in England. *British Medical Journal, 325*,

1207-1211.

Heath, N.L., Toste, J.R., Nedecheva, T., Charlebois, A., 2008. An examination of nonsuicidal

self-injury among college students. *Journal of Mental Health Counseling, 30*, 137–156.

Herpertz, S., Sass, H., & Favazza, A. (1997). Impulsivity in self-mutilative behavior:

Psychometric and biological findings. *Journal of Psychiatric Research, 31*(4), 451-465.

Herpretz, S. (2995). Self-injurious behavior: Psychopathological and nosological

characteristics in subtypes in self-injurers. *Acta Psychiatrica Scandinavica, 91*, 57-68.

Horesh, N., Gothelf, D., Ofek, H., Weizman, T., & Apter, A. (1999). Impulsivity as a correlate

of suicidal behavior in adolescent psychiatric inpatients. *Crisis, 20*(1), 8-14.

Jacobson, C. M., & Gould, M. (2007). The epidemiology and phenomenology of non-suicidal

self-injurious behavior among adolescents: A critical review of the literature. *Archives of

Suicide Research, 11*, 129-147.

Jarvis, G. K., Ferrence, R. G., Johnson, F. G., & Whitehead, P. C. (1976). Sex and age

patterns   in self-injury. *Journal of Health and Social Behavior, 17*, 146-155.

Jones, I. H., & Daniels, B. A. (1996). An ethological approach to self-injury. *British Journal

of Psychiatry, 169*, 263-267.

Keuthen, N. J., Deckersbach, T., Wilhelm, S., Hale, E., Fraim, C., Baer, L., O'Sullivan, R. L.,

& Jenike, M. A. (2000). Repetitive skin-picking in a student population and comparison

with a sample of self-injurious skin-pickers. *Psychosomatics, 41*(3), 210-215.

Kim, C., Lesage, A., Seguin, M., Lipp. O., Vanier, C., & Turecki, G. (2003). Patterns of

comobidity in male suicide completers. *Psychological Medicine, 33*, 1299-1309.

Klonsky, E. D. (2007). The functions of deliberate self-injury: A review of the evidence.

*Clinical Psychology Review, 27*, 226-239.

Klonsky, E.D., Oltmanns, T. F., & Turkheimer, E. (2003). Deliberate self-harm in a

nonclinical population: Prevalence and psychological correlates. American *Journal of*

*Psychiatry, 160*(8), 1501-1508.

Kumar, G., Pepe, D., & Steer, R. A. (2004). Adolescent psychiatric inpatients' self-reported

reasons for cutting themselves. *The Journal of Nervous and Mental Disease, 192*(12),

830-836.

Latalova, K., & Prasko, J. (2010). Aggression in borderline personality disorder. *Psychiatric*

*Quarterly, 81*, 239-251.

Laye-Gindhu, A., & Schonert-Reichl, K. A. (2005). Nonsuicidal Self-Harm Among

Community Adolescents: Understanding the "Whats" and "Whys" of Self-Harm.

*Journal of Youth and Adolescence, 34*, 447-457.

Lochner, C., Simeon, D., Nichaus, D. H., & Stein, D. J. (2002). Trichotillomania and

skin-picking: A phenomenological comparison. *Depression and Anxiety, 15*, 83-86.

Lutz, C., Marinus, L., Chase, W., Meyer, J., & Novak, M. (2003), Self-injurious behavior

in ,male rhesus macaques does not reflect externally directed aggression. *Physiology*

*and Behavior, 78*, 33-39.

Matsumoto, T., Yamaguchi, A., Chiba, Y., Asami, T., Iseki, E., & Hirayasu, Y. (2004).

Patterns of self-cutting: A preliminary study on differences in clinical implications between srist- and arm- cutting using a Japanese juvenile detention center sample.

*Psychiatry and Clinical Neuroscience, 58*, 377-382.

Milligan, R. J., & Waller, G. (2001). Anger and impulsivity in non-clinical women.

*Personality and Individual Differences, 30*, 1073-1078.

Milnes, D., Owens, D., & Blenkiron, P. (2002). Problems reported by self-harm patients:

Perception, hopelessness, and suicidal intent. *Journal of Psychosomatic Research, 53*,

819-822.

Moscicki, E. K. (1994). Gender differences in completed and attempted suicides. *Annals of*

*Epidemiology, 4*, 152 -158.

Neziroglu, F., & Mancebo, M. (2001). Skin picking as a form of self-injurious behavior.

*Psychiatric Annals, 31*(9), 549-555.

Nock, M. K. (2010). Self-injury. *Annual Review of Clinical Osychology, 6*, 339-363.

Nock, M. K., & Marzuk, P. M. (2000). Suicide and violence. In K. Hawton & K. Van

Heeringen (Eds.), *The International Handbook of Suicide and Attempted Suicde* (pp.

437-456). Chichester: Wiley.

Nock, M. K., & Mendes, W. B. (2008). Physiological arousal, distress tolerance, and social

problem-solving deficits among adolescents self-injurers. *Journal of Consulting and*

*Clinical Psychology, 76*(1), 28-38.

Nock, M. K., & Prinstein, M. J. (2004). A functional approach to the assessment of self-mutilative behavior. *Journal of Consulting and Clinical Psychology, 72*(5), 885-890.

Nock, M. K. (2009) Why do people hurt themselves? New insights into the nature and

function of self-injury. *Current Directions in Psychologcial Science, 18*, 78-83.

Nock, M. K., Joiner Jr, T. E., Gordon, K. H., Lloyd-Richardson, E., & Prinstein, M. J. (2006).

Non-suicidal self-injury among adolescents: *Diagnostic correlates and relation to*

*suicide attempts. Psychiatry Research, 144*, 65-72.

Hilt, L. M., Cha, C. B., & Nolen-Hoeksema, S. (2008). Non-suicidal self-injury in young

adolescent girls: Moderators of the distress-function relationship. *Journal of Consulting*

*Clincial Psychology, 76*, 63-71.

O'Connor, R. C., Rasmussen, S., & Hawton, K. (2009). Predicting deliberate self-harm in

adolescents: A six month prospective study. *Suicide and Life-Threatening Behavior,*

*39*(4), 364-375.

Parker, J. D. A., Bagby, R. M., & Webster, C. D. (1993). Domains of the impulsivity

construct: A factor analytic investigation. *Personality and Individual Differences, 15*,

267-274.

Patton, G. C., Hemphill, S. A., Beyers, J. M., Bond, L., Toumbourou, J. W., McMorris, B. J.,

& Catalano, R. F. (2007). Pubertal stage and deliberate self-harm in adolescents. *Journal*

*of American Academy of Child and Adolescent Psychiatry, 46*(4), 508-514.

Portzky, G., & Heeringen, K. van. (2007). Deliberate self-harm in adolescents. *Current*

*Opinion in Psychiatry, 20,* 337-342.

Ross, S., & Heath, N. (2002). A study of the frequency of self-mutilation in a community

sample of adolescents. *Journal of Youth and Adolescents, 31*(1), 67-77.

Ross, S., & Heath, N. L. (2003). Two models of adolescents self-mutilation. *Suicide &*

*Life-Threatening Behavior, 33*(3), 277-287.

Sakelliadis, E. I., Papadodima, S. A., Sergentanis, T. N., Giotakos, O., Spiliopoulou, C. A.

(2009). Self-injurious behavior among Greek male prisoners: Prevalence and risk

factors. *European Psychiatry, 25,* 151-158.

Schroeder, S. R., Mulick, J. A., & Rojahn, J. (1980). The definition, taxonomy, epidemiology

and ecology of self-injurious behavior. *Journal of Autism and Developmental*

*Disorders, 10*(4), 417-432.

Simeon, D., Stanley, B., Frances, A., Mann, J. J., Winchel, R., & Stanley, M. (1992).

Self-mutilation in personality disorders: Psychological and biological correlates. *The*

*American Journal of Psychiatry, 149*(2), 221-226.

Soloff, P. H., Lis, J. A., Kelly, T., Cornelius, J., & Ulrich, R. (1994). Risk factors for suicidal

behaviors in borderline personality disorder. *American Journal of Psychiatry, 149,*

221-226.

Standford, S., & Jones, M. P. (2009). Psychological subtyping finds pathological, impulsive,

and "normal" groups among adolescents who-self-harm. *Journal of Child Psychology and Psychiatry, 50*(7), 807-815.

Stanley, B., Gameroff, M., Michalsen, V., & Mann, J. J. (2001). Are suicide attempters who

self-mutilate a unique population?. *The American Journal of Psychiatry, 158*(3),

427-432.

Suyemoto, K. L., & Macdonald, M. L. (1995). Self-cutting in female adolescents.

*Psychotherapy, 32*(1), 162-171.

Suyemoto, K. L. (1998). The functions of self-mutilation. *Clinical Psychology Review,*

*18*(5), 531–554.

Swenson, L., Spirito, A., Dyl, J., Kitter, J., & Hunt, J. I. (2008). Psychiatric correlates of

nonsuicidal cutting behaviors in an adolescent inpatient sample. *Child Psychiatry*

*Human Development, 39*, 427-438.

Thombs, B. D., Bresnick, M. G., & Magyar-Russel, G. (2007). Who attempts suicide by

burning? An analysis of age patterns of mortality by self-inflicting burning in the United

States. *General Hospital Psychiatry, 29*, 244-250.

Tuisku, V., Pelkonen, M., Kiviruusu, O., Karlsson, L., Ruuttu, T., & Marttunen, M. (2009).

Factors associated with deliberate self-harm behavior among depressed adolescent

outpatients. *Journal of Adolescence, 32*, 1125-1136.

Van Orden, K.A., Merrill, K.A., & Joiner, T.E. (2005) Interpersonal-psychological precursors

to suicidal behavior: A theory of attempted and completed suicide. *Current*

*Psychiatry Reviews, 1,* 187-196.

Weissman, M. M. (1974). The epidemiology of suicide attempts, 1960-1971. *Archives of*

*General Psychiatry, 20,* 737-746.

Wilhelm, S., Keuthen, N. J., Deckersbach, T., Enhelhard, I. M., Forker, A. E., Baer, L.,

O'Sullivan, R. L., & Jenike, M. A. (1999). *Journal of Clinical Psychiatry, 60*(7),

454-459.

Wong, J. P. S., Stewart, S. M., Ho, S. Y., & Lam, T. H. (2007). Risk factors associated

with suicide attempts and other self-injury among Hong Kong adolescents. *Suicide and*

*Life-Threatening Behavior, 37,* 453-466.

Yip, K. S. (2005). A multi-dimensional perspective of adolescents' self-cutting. *Child and*

*Adolescent Mental Health, 10*(2), 80-86.

0  1341  1485033  9

CPSIA information can be obtained at www.ICGtesting.com
Printed in the USA
LVOW041215021212

309744LV00005B/787/P

9  783845  477312